Pre-Reader Bible Story Leaflets **FALL Year 1**

Bible Story Basics: Building a Better World Through Story

Hello!

You're holding in your hands the BIBLE STORY BASICS: PRE-READER, BIBLE STORY LEAFLETS. These leaflets help you tell your children the Bible story in words that they will understand. These leaflets are helpful for in-classroom learning, and they serve as take-home leaflets for families.

Each story has an element to engage your children actively. It might be a motion or a repetitive word, or it might be identifying a particular Bible character. The stories are designed to introduce your children to the Bible, in order to build a foundation that will grow and last a lifetime.

These leaflets also encourage parents and caregivers to continue exploring the Bible story at home throughout the week, using the conversation suggestions provided—at family dinners, in the car, and at bedtime.

We hope that you'll find the Bible Story Basics Leaflets helpful as you minister to your children and share God's love with these precious children of God.

Daphna Flegal, Bible Story Basics Editor

TO FIND OUT MORE, visit
biblestorybasics.com.

Fall Year 1
Table of Contents

Session 1	Creation
Parent Take-Home	Using the Bible at Home
Session 2	God's Image
Session 3	Adam and Eve
Session 4	Noah
Session 5	Tower of Babel
Session 6	Abraham and Sarah
Session 7	Abraham and Lot
Session 8	The Birth of Isaac
Session 9	Isaac and Rebekah
Session 10	Jacob and Esau
Session 11	The Birthright
Session 12	The Blessing
Session 13	Jacob's Dream
Thanksgiving Send-Home	Happy Thanksgiving!
Songbook Take-Home	Bible Story Basics Songbook

Creation

Add stars all around the earth.

Talk About It

Use these questions to talk about today's Bible story with your child.

- What do we do when it is daytime? What's in the sky when it's day?
- What do we do when it is nighttime? What's in the sky when it's night?

PRAY: Thank you, God, for all the wonderful things you have made. Amen.

Pre-Reader • **Session 1** • Fall Year 1

Creation | Genesis 1:1-25

God saw everything he had made: it was supremely good.

Genesis 1:31

Bible Story Basics

biblestorybasics.com

Creation

In the beginning, there was nothing. *(Shake your head no.)*

God said, "Let there be light." And light appeared. *(Flick your hands above your head.)* God divided the light from the darkness. God called the light Day. God called the darkness Night. *(Flick one hand above your head, then flick your other hand above your head.)* And that all happened on day number one. *(Hold up one finger.)*

On day number two… *(Hold up two fingers.)* God made the sky. *(Sweep one arm over your head.)*

On day number three… *(Hold up three fingers.)* God divided the land from the water. God called the land Earth. God called the water Seas. *(Hold both hands together, palms facing the floor, then separate your hands to either side.)* Then God made seeds and plants and trees. *(Sway your arms like a tree in the wind.)*

On day number four… *(Hold up four fingers.)* God made the sun and the moon and the stars. *(Make a circle with your hands over your head.)*

On day number five… *(Hold up five fingers.)* God made fish to swim in the seas *(Hold your palms together, and wiggle your hands like a fish.)* and birds to fly in the sky. *(Flap your arms like wings.)*

On day number six… *(Hold up six fingers.)* God made animals—animals that make fun noises, like cows and sheep *(Say, "Moo. Baa.")*; animals that crawl, like lizards and snakes *(Crawl.)*; and animals that live in the wild, like tigers and bears. *(Growl.)*

God looked at all the things that God had made on days one, two, three, four, five, and six. *(Hold up one, two, three, four, five, and six fingers.)*

And God saw that it was good.

Holy Bible

Color the Bible.

Talk About It

Use these questions to talk about the Bible with your child.

- What is your favorite Bible story?
- What's one thing you know about Jesus?

PRAY: Thank you, God, for the Bible. Amen.

Pre-Reader • **Parent Take-Home** • Fall Year 1

Using the Bible at Home

Everybody who hears these words of mine and puts them into practice is like a wise builder who built a house on bedrock.

Matthew 7:24

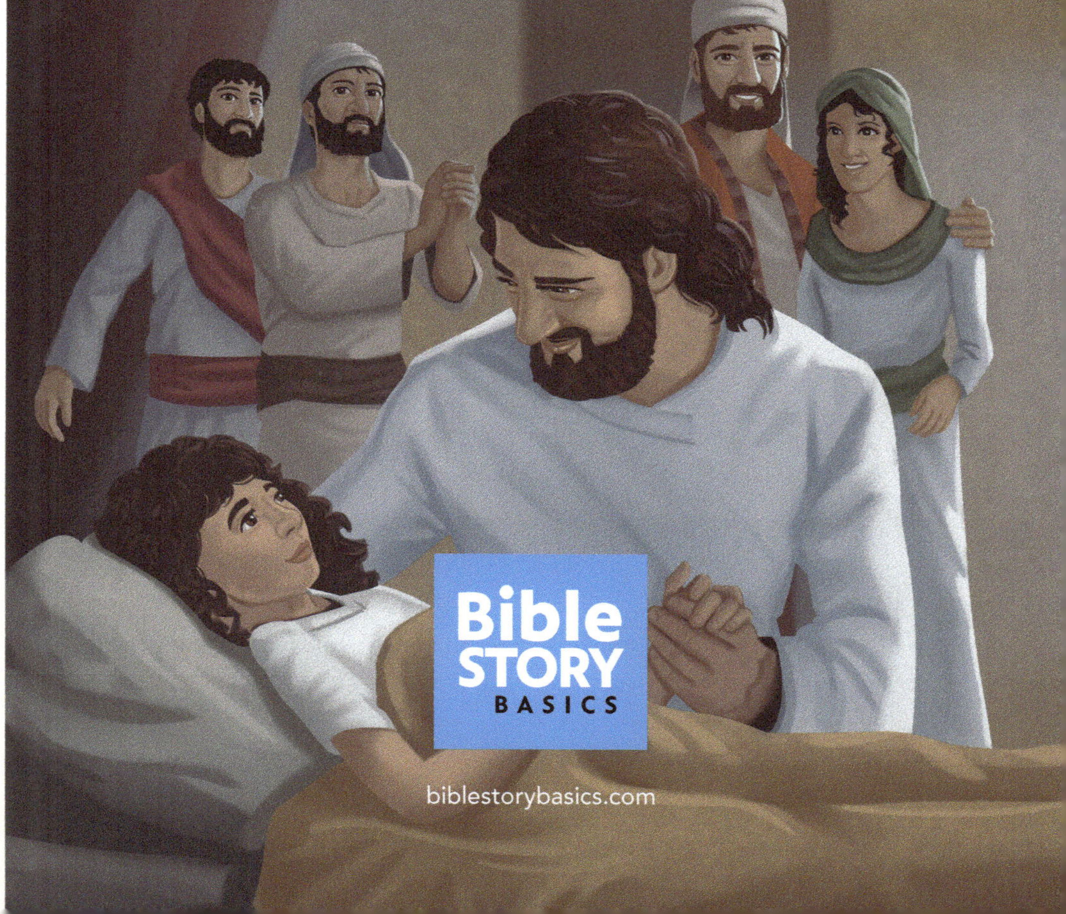

Bible STORY BASICS

biblestorybasics.com

Using the Bible at Home

The Bible is a collection of stories that tell of God, Jesus, and God's people.

Your church has chosen Bible Story Basics as the curriculum for your child. This curriculum will help your child interact with the Bible on his or her level.

Your child will learn that the Old Testament introduces us to God and the many people through whom God chose to work. These people listened to God, even though they often made mistakes, argued with their brothers and sisters, moved from place to place, and went through many hard times. God loved these people, and the people continued to love God.

Constantly remind your child that God is always with us and that God always loves us.

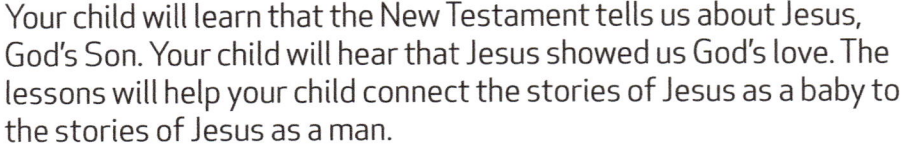

Your child will learn that the New Testament tells us about Jesus, God's Son. Your child will hear that Jesus showed us God's love. The lessons will help your child connect the stories of Jesus as a baby to the stories of Jesus as a man.

Above all, the stories are opportunities to remind your child that Jesus loves us all.

Your child also will learn that the New Testament contains stories of the people who became followers of Jesus.

These stories remind us of how we can live as followers of Jesus.

Each month, your child will hear a Bible verse that connects to the Bible stories. Help your child repeat and remember the verse. Young children will remember the verse best when they have the opportunity to say, sing, play, draw, and dance the verse. These experiences will be offered in each week's lesson. You can reinforce these activities at home.

Use the Bible at home. Let your child see you reading the Bible. Handle the Bible with care and place it in a special spot in your home. Read to your child from the Bible, a Bible storybook, and each week's leaflet. Open your family's Bible and show your child where the story is found as you read from a Bible storybook or the leaflet.

Ask your child wondering questions about each story. "How do you think Noah felt when it started to rain?" "How do you think Mary felt when the angel said her name?" "How would you feel if you saw an angel?" There are no right or wrong answers to these kinds of questions.

Enjoy reading the Bible, exploring God's Word, and learning the Bible stories as a family.

God Made Me

Color the face below to be like you.

Talk About It

Use these questions to talk about today's Bible story with your child.

- What are three things you like about how you look?
- What are three things you like about how you act?

PRAY: Thank you, God, for making us in your image. Amen.

God's Image

On days number one, two, three, four, and five... *(Hold up one, two, three, four, and five fingers.)* God made the earth, the sky, the plants, the fish, and the birds.

On day number six... *(Hold up six fingers.)* God made all the animals.

And on day number six, God made something else—God made another creation.

This creation had two legs and two feet. *(Shake your legs.)*

This creation had two arms and two hands. *(Shake your arms.)*

This creation had two eyes and two ears. *(Point to your eyes, then point to your ears.)*

This creation had one nose and one mouth. *(Point to your nose, then point to your mouth.)*

This creation was—people!

And while the people had some things that were the same—like legs and feet and arms and hands and eyes and ears and noses and mouths *(Shake your legs and arms, then point to your eyes, ears, nose, and mouth.)*—the people had other things that were different, like the color of their hair, how fast they could run, and the foods they liked. But no matter what, the people were all part of God's creation.

God made people in the image of God. That means that all people have some things that are like God.

All people have hearts to love *(Cross your hands over your heart.)* and brains to think. *(Point to your head.)*

All people can take care of the earth *(Make a large circle with your arms.)* and take care of one another. *(Hug yourself.)*

God looked around at everything God had made. *(Look around.)* God knew that everything was very good. *(Nod your head yes.)*

Then on day number seven... *(Hold up seven fingers.)* God rested. *(Sit down.)*

The Garden

Find a crescent moon, a star, a flower, a sprouting tree with one tiny leaf, and an acorn hidden in the picture below.

Talk About It

Use these questions to talk about today's Bible story with your child.

- How do you think Adam and Eve felt when they had to leave the garden?
- Who helps you make good choices?

PRAY: Thank you, God, for always loving us. Amen.

Pre-Reader • Session 3 • Fall Year 1

Adam and Eve
Genesis 2:4b–3:24

God saw everything he had made: it was supremely good.
Genesis 1:31

Bible Story Basics

biblestorybasics.com

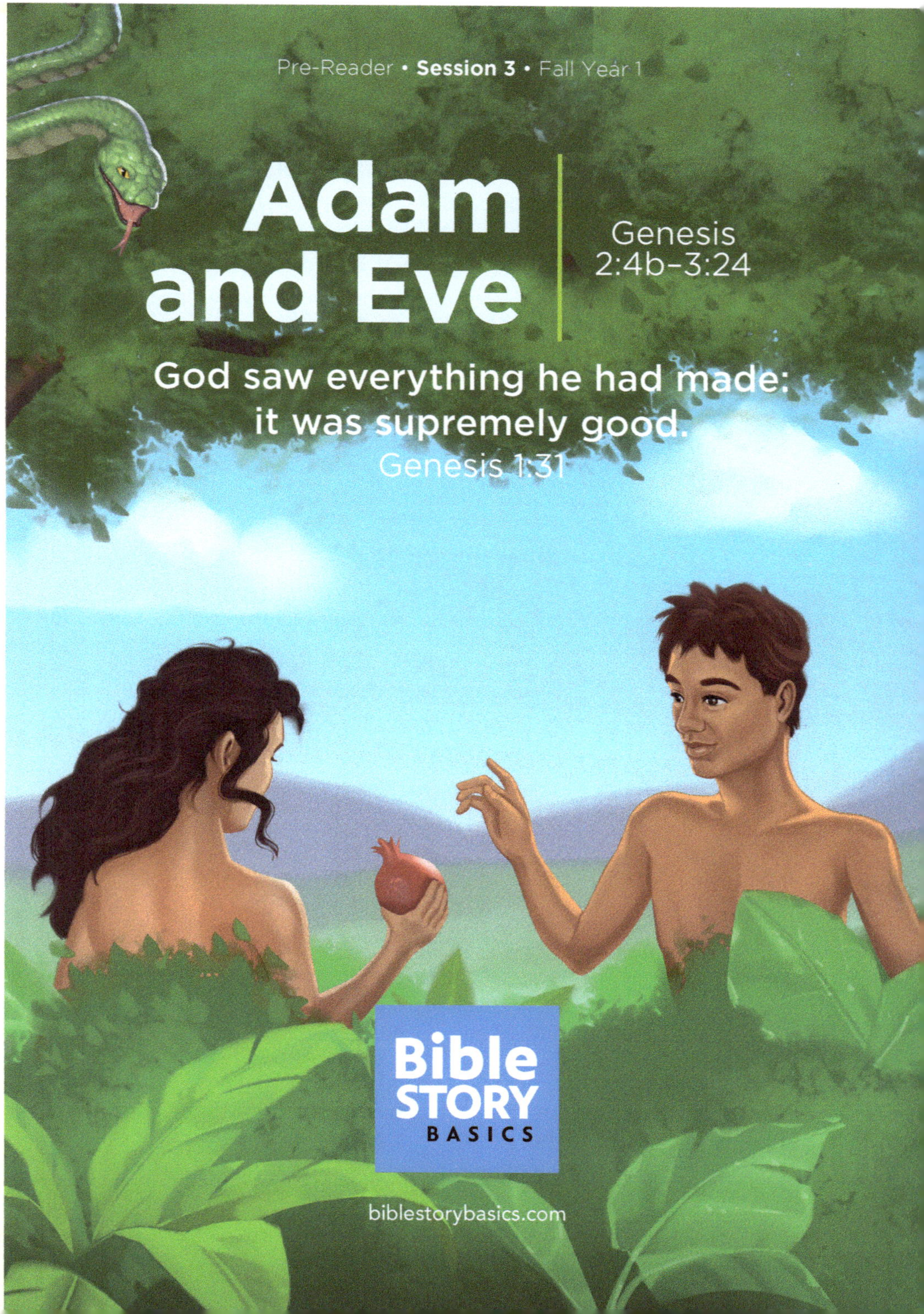

Adam and Eve

God made a man and named him Adam. God blew breath into Adam, and he came to life. *(Blow.)*

God made a beautiful garden. The garden had many beautiful trees. *(Wave your arms like tree branches.)*

"You may eat any of the fruit in the garden," God told Adam *(Nod your head yes.)*, "except for the fruit from the tree of the knowledge of good and evil." *(Shake your head no.)* "You must not eat that fruit."

Then God made wild animals *(Hold your hands like claws and growl.)* and birds. *(Flap your arms.)* God wanted Adam to name each animal.

Adam named the lion *(Pretend to roar.)*, the duck *(Say, "Quack, quack.")*, and the sheep. *(Say, "Baa, baa.")* Adam named all the animals.

But Adam was lonely. So, God made a woman named Eve. Now there were two people—Adam *(Hold out one hand.)* and Eve. *(Hold out the other hand.)*

Adam and Eve lived happily together in the garden. They ate the fruit of all the trees *(Pretend to eat.)*, except for the tree of the knowledge of good and evil. *(Shake your head no.)*

One day, Eve heard an animal speak to her. It was a snake. *(Pretend to hiss.)*

"You should eat the fruit from this s-s-special tree," said the snake. The snake wanted Eve to eat from the tree of the knowledge of good and evil. *(Cover your mouth with your hands.)*

"I can't," said Eve. "God told us to never eat that fruit." *(Shake your head no.)*

"Yes-s-s, you can," said the snake. *(Pretend to hiss.)* "It won't hurt you."

So, Eve chose to eat the fruit. Then she chose to give Adam some of the fruit, and he chose to eat it, too. *(Pretend to eat.)*

Adam and Eve immediately knew they had made a bad choice! *(Cover your mouth with your hands.)*

God found Adam and Eve in the garden. "You disobeyed me," said God. "Now you must leave this beautiful garden." *(Point away.)*

God was sorry that Adam and Eve had to leave the garden. Even though Adam and Eve made a bad choice, God still loved them and cared for them. *(Cross your hands over your heart.)*

Two of Every Creature

God told Noah to bring two of every animal onto the ark. Match each animal with the food the animal eats.

Talk About It

Use these questions to talk about today's Bible story with your child.

- How do you think Noah felt when he had all the animals on the ark?
- How do you feel when you see a rainbow?

PRAY: Thank you, God, for promising to take care of the earth. Amen.

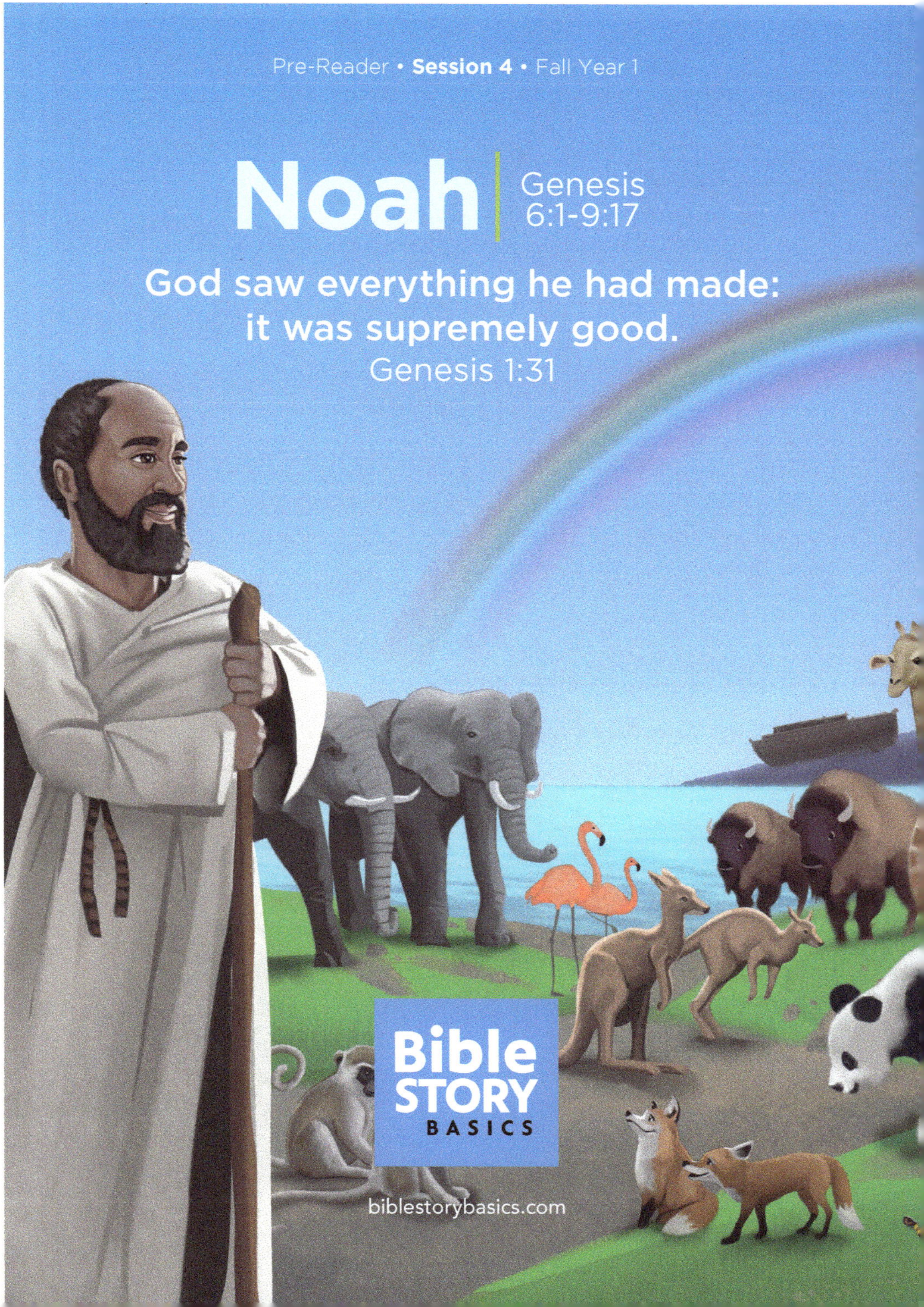

Noah

"Noah!" God called. "I want you to build a big, big, BIG boat." *(Spread your arms wide.)* Noah listened to God. He built a big, big, BIG boat. *(Spread your arms wide.)*

"Noah!" God called. "I want you to bring two of every kind of animal into the big, big, BIG boat." *(Spread your arms wide.)*

Noah listened to God. He gathered two of every kind of animal into the big, big, BIG boat. *(Spread your arms wide.)*

Baa, baa—two sheep. Chee, chee—two monkeys. Hiss, hiss—two snakes. And many, many more animals. When Noah finished rounding up the animals, Noah, his wife, his sons, and their wives all got on the big, big, BIG boat. *(Spread your arms wide.)*

Slam! *(Clap your hands once.)* God shut the door of the big, big, BIG boat. *(Spread your arms wide.)*

Soon it started to rain. It rained and rained and rained. The big, big, BIG boat started to float. *(Spread your arms wide.)*

It rained for forty days and forty nights. But Noah, his family, and all the animals were safe on the big, big, BIG boat. *(Spread your arms wide.)* Then the rain stopped. The boat landed on top of a mountain.

Caw, caw. *(Flap your arms like a bird.)* Noah sent a raven to see if it was safe to leave the big, big, BIG boat. *(Spread your arms wide.)*

But the raven came back, so it was not safe yet.

Coo, coo. *(Flap your arms like a bird.)* Noah sent a dove to see if it was safe to leave the big, big, BIG boat. *(Spread your arms wide.)*

But the dove came back, so it was not safe yet.

Noah waited several more days. Then he sent the dove out again. The dove did not come back! It was safe to leave the big, big, BIG boat. *(Spread your arms wide.)*

Noah, his family, and all the animals left the big, big, BIG boat. *(Spread your arms wide.)*

Noah build an altar to thank God for keeping them safe. *(Fold your hands in prayer.)*

Then a rainbow appeared in the sky. Noah looked at all the colors of the rainbow and knew that God loved him. *(Cross your hands over your heart.)*

Different Is Good

The children below are different from one another. Match each child with the correct shadow. God planned for people to be different.

Talk About It

Use these questions to talk about today's Bible story with your child.

- How are you the same as your friends? How are you different?
- Do you know someone who speaks a language that is different from your own? How do you feel when you hear that person speak?

PRAY: Thank you, God, for all the ways we are the same and all the ways we are different. Amen.

Pre-Reader • **Session 5** • Fall Year 1

Tower of Babel
Genesis 11:1-9

God saw everything he had made: it was supremely good.
Genesis 1:31

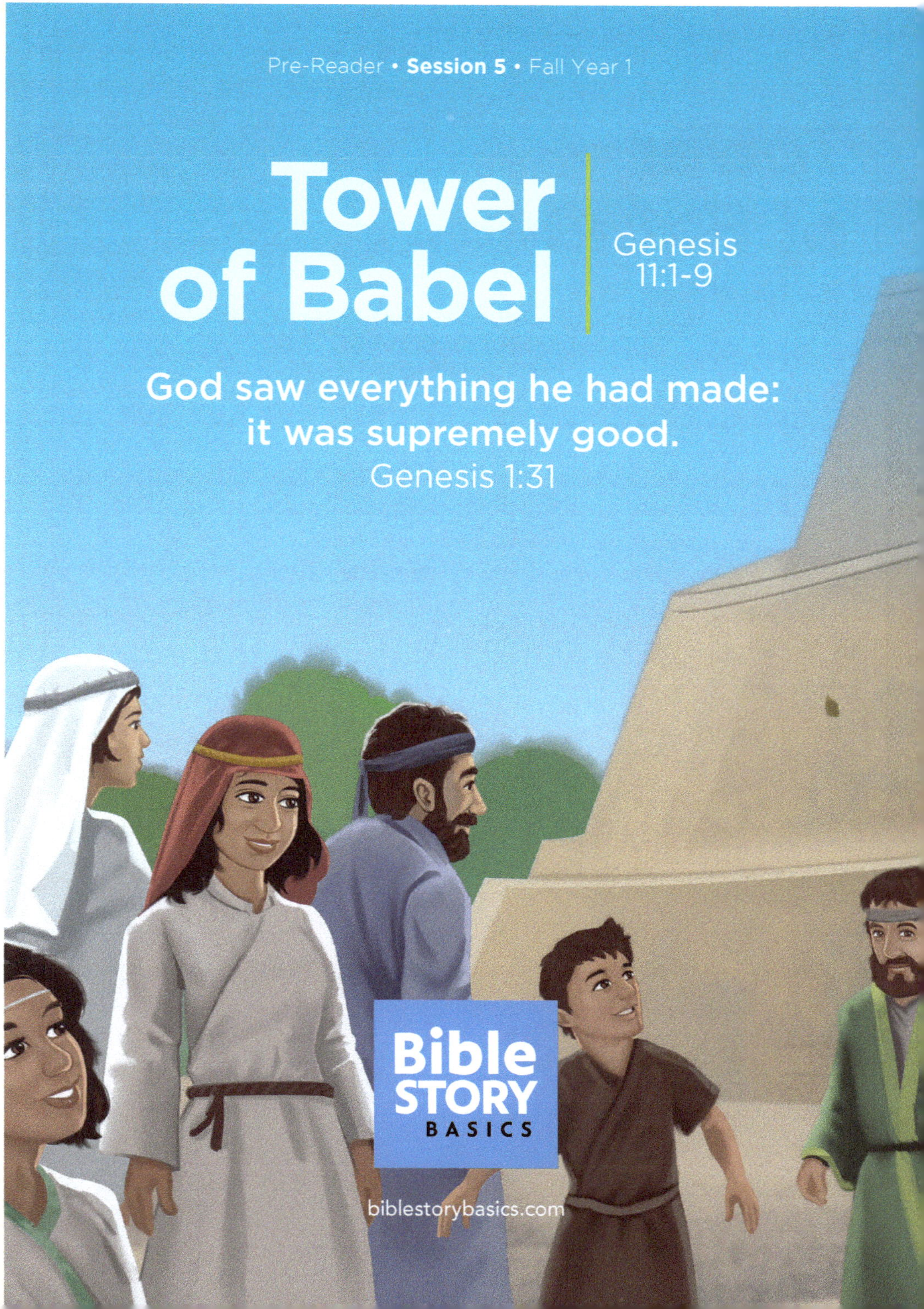

Bible Story Basics

biblestorybasics.com

Tower of Babel

A long time ago, all the people of the world spoke the same language and used the same words. It was easy for them to talk to one another.

"Hi! Howdy! Hello!"

The people wanted to live together in the same place. They decided that they would work together to build one city with a tall, tall tower.

First, the people made bricks. Then they used the bricks to build the tall tower.

They made the first layer of bricks. *(Crouch down near the floor.)*

Then they added more bricks, layer after layer. *(Slowly straighten up.)*

They wanted the tower to be the tallest tower in the world. *(Stand up straight with your arms stretched above your head.)*

They wanted the tower to reach the sky. *(Stand on your tiptoes with your arms stretched above your head.)*

But God did not want the people to live in one city. God wanted the people to live in different places all over the earth. *(Shake your head no.)*

So, God created new and different languages for all the people. Now the people could not talk to one another.

"Hola? *(oh-lah)* **Jambo?** *(jahm-boh)* **Hello?"**

The people got tired of trying to build the tower. They left the tower and went to live in different places, just as God wanted them to do.

The tower was never finished. It was called Babel. That name was chosen because it means "confusing talk."

"Babel, Babel, Babel."

What's Different?

Find five things in the picture on the bottom that are different from the picture on the top.

Talk About It

Use these questions to talk about today's Bible story with your child.

- Have you ever moved to a new place? How did you feel?
- How do you think Abraham and Sarah felt when they moved to a new place?

PRAY: Thank you, God, for being with us no matter where we go. Amen.

Pre-Reader • **Session 6** • Fall Year 1

Abraham and Sarah

Genesis 12:1-9; 15:1-6

Look up at the sky and count the stars... This is how many children you will have.

Genesis 15:5

Bible STORY BASICS

biblestorybasics.com

Abraham and Sarah

"Abraham, Abraham!" called God. *(Cup your hands around your mouth.)*

"I want you to pack up your whole family and move to a different place." *(Walk in place.)*

"Listen to me and I will tell you where to go." *(Keep walking; cup your hands around your ears.)*

Abraham did what God told him to do. *(Stop walking; cross your hands over your heart.)*

Abraham, his wife Sarah, and his nephew Lot moved their tents, their sheep, and their goats to a new place. *(Walk in place.)*

God promised Abraham and Sarah that they would have many grandchildren and great-grandchildren and great-great-grandchildren. *(Stop walking; cross your hands over your heart.)*

But how could that be? Abraham and Sarah had no children. *(Shrug your shoulders; shake your head no.)*

Then Abraham had a dream. *(Press your hands together, and rest your cheek on your hands.)*

"Don't be afraid, Abraham," said God. *(Shake your head no.)*

"I am with you. I will give you a big family, just as I promised." *(Cross your hands over your heart.)*

"Look up at the night sky." *(Look up.)*

"Can you count the stars?" asked God. "That's how many people will be in your big family." *(Pretend to point to several different stars.)*

Abraham looked up at all the stars. There were too many stars to count. *(Keep pointing to the stars.)*

When Abraham saw the stars, he knew he could trust God. *(Cross your hands over your heart.)*

Abraham and Lot Go Different Ways

This maze has two paths. Follow the path from Abraham to Abraham and the path from Lot to Lot.

Talk About It

Use these questions to talk about today's Bible story with your child.

- How were Abraham and Lot peacemakers?
- How can you be a peacemaker?

PRAY: Dear God, help us be peacemakers and share with one another. Amen.

Abraham and Lot

Abraham and Sarah continued to move where God told them to go. *(Walk in place.)*

Abraham's nephew Lot moved with them. *(Walk in place.)*

Abraham, Sarah, and Lot took all their sheep *(Say, "Baa.")* with them as they moved from place to place. Finally, they stopped at a place called Bethel.

Abraham and Lot both had lots of sheep. *(Say, "Baa.")* They had so many sheep *(Say, "Baa.")* that there was not enough grass for all the animals to eat.

The shepherds taking care of Abraham's animals and the shepherds taking care of Lot's animals began to fight. *(Hold your hands in fists.)*

Abraham's shepherds said to Lot's shepherds, "Hey, get out of here! This grass is for my sheep." *(Say, "Baa.")*

"It is not!" said Lot's shepherds to Abraham's shepherds. "The grass is for my sheep." *(Say, "Baa.")*

Abraham and Lot did not want their shepherds to fight with one another. *(Shake your head no.)*

But there just wasn't enough grass for all the animals to eat. What could they do? *(Shrug your shoulders.)*

"Let's not fight," said Abraham to Lot. "Let's move to different parts of the land. If you go that way *(Point away from yourself.)*, I'll go that way. *(Point in the opposite direction.)*

"That's a good idea," said Lot. Lot looked around at the land. He saw a beautiful valley with plenty of grass for his sheep. *(Say, "Baa.")*

"I'll go this way," said Lot. *(Point away from yourself.)*

"Fine," said Abraham. "Then I'll go that way." *(Point in the opposite direction.)*

So, Abraham and Lot moved away from each other. *(Walk in place.)*

Abraham and Lot found a peaceful solution to the fight. *(Cross your hands over your heart.)*

Take Care of Baby Isaac

Circle the Bible-times items Sarah and Abraham can use to take care of baby Isaac.

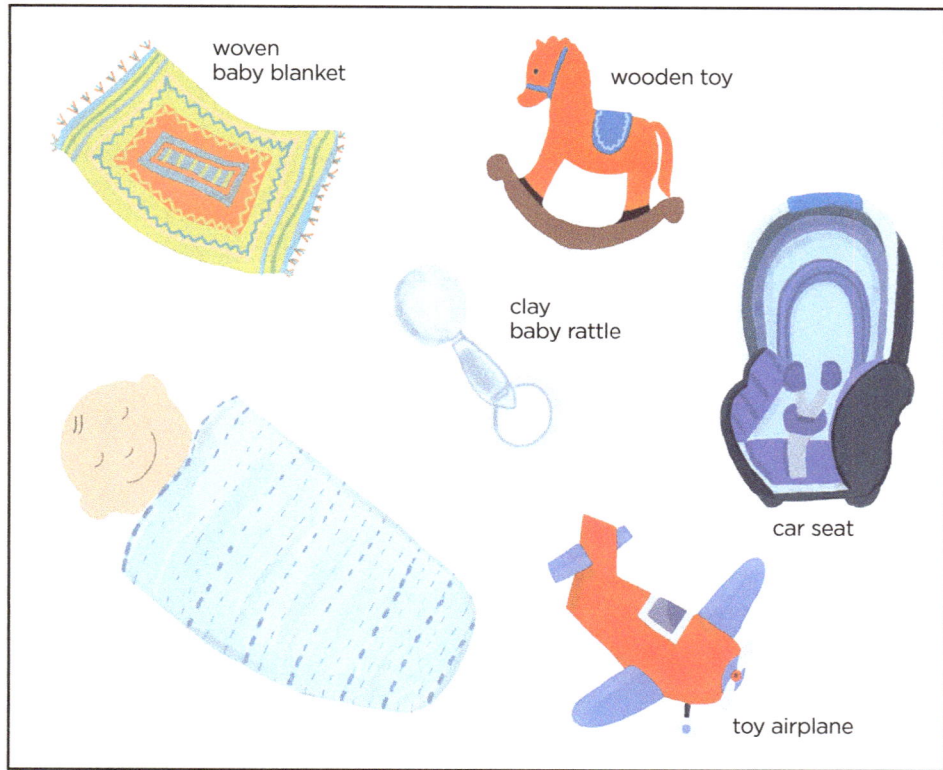

- woven baby blanket
- wooden toy
- clay baby rattle
- car seat
- toy airplane

Talk About It

Use these questions to talk about today's Bible story with your child.

- How do you think Sarah felt when she gave birth to baby Isaac?
- God kept the promise. Baby Isaac was the start of a big family for Abraham and Sarah. How do you feel when someone makes a promise to you? How do you feel when someone keeps the promise?

PRAY: Thank you, God, for keeping your promise. Amen.

Pre-Reader • **Session 8** • Fall Year 1

The Birth of Isaac

Genesis 18:1-15; 21:1-7

Look up at the sky and count the stars...
This is how many children you will have.
Genesis 15:5

Bible STORY BASICS

biblestorybasics.com

The Birth of Isaac

God promised Abraham and Sarah that they would have a big family.

"Ha, ha, ha!" *(Pretend to laugh.)*

But many years had passed, and they still did not have a child. Sarah was too old to have a baby.

"Ha, ha, ha!" *(Pretend to laugh.)*

Abraham was outside one day when he saw three visitors coming toward him. Abraham welcomed the visitors. He ran to Sarah and asked her to make bread for the visitors to eat.

"Ha, ha, ha!" *(Pretend to laugh.)*

Sarah made the bread. Abraham sat with the three visitors while they ate. Sarah stood inside the tent, listening to the men.

"Ha, ha, ha!" *(Pretend to laugh.)*

"Next year, your wife Sarah will have a son," said one of the men.

"Ha, ha, ha!" *(Pretend to laugh.)*

Sarah laughed! She was too old to have a baby.

"Ha, ha, ha!" *(Pretend to laugh.)*

But one year later, Sarah gave birth to a baby boy. Sarah and Abraham named the baby Isaac. The name *Isaac* means "He laughs."

"Ha, ha, ha!" *(Pretend to laugh.)*

"Now I am laughing with joy," said Sarah happily. "I have a son!"

"Ha, ha, ha!" *(Pretend to laugh.)*

God kept the promise. Isaac was the beginning of Abraham and Sarah's big family.

Find a Wife for Isaac

Help Abraham's servant find his way to Rebekah.

Talk About It

Use these questions to talk about today's Bible story with your child.

• Who helped the servant find a wife for Isaac?

• How do you think Isaac and Rebekah felt when they got married?

PRAY: Thank you, God, for listening to us when we pray. Amen.

Pre-Reader • **Session 9** • Fall Year 1

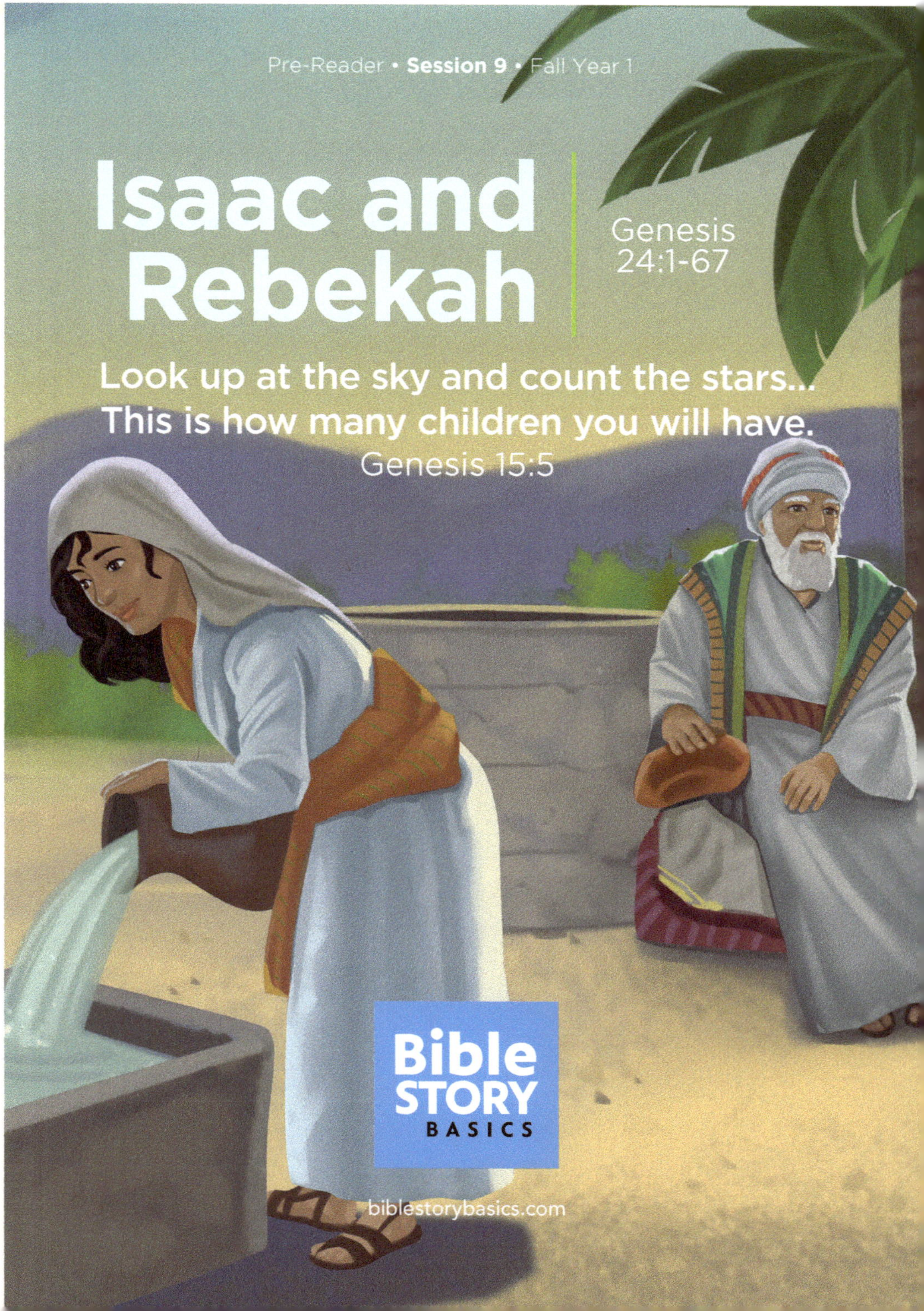

Isaac and Rebekah
Genesis 24:1-67

Look up at the sky and count the stars...
This is how many children you will have.
Genesis 15:5

Bible STORY BASICS

biblestorybasics.com

Isaac and Rebekah

Isaac grew from a baby to a man. *(Crouch down, then stand up tall.)*

One day, Isaac's dad, Abraham, called his servant. *(Cup your hands around your mouth.)*

"It's time for Isaac to marry," Abraham said to the servant. "Go to my family's homeland and find a wife for Isaac." *(Point away from yourself.)*

So, the servant took ten camels *(Hold up ten fingers.)* and traveled to the city where Abraham's family lived. *(Walk in place.)*

It was a long trip. *(Keep walking in place.)*

Finally, the servant and all the camels stopped at a well just outside the city. *(Stop walking.)*

"Oh, God," the servant prayed, "help me. Show me the woman you want Isaac to marry." *(Fold your hands in prayer.)*

Soon, a young woman named Rebekah came to the well to get water. *(Walk in place.)*

"May I have a drink of your water?" asked the servant. *(Pretend to drink.)*

"Of course," said Rebekah. "I'll also get water for your ten camels." *(Hold up ten fingers.)*

This is the woman God wants Isaac to marry, thought the servant. *(Tap your finger on the side of your head.)*

The servant went with Rebekah to meet Rebekah's family. *(Walk in place.)*

"God has chosen Rebekah to be the wife of Abraham's son Isaac," the servant said to Rebekah's family. *(Cross your hands over your heart.)*

"Will you let me take her home to marry Isaac?" he asked. *(Point away from yourself.)*

"Yes," answered Rebekah's family. Rebekah agreed. *(Nod your head yes.)*

So, Rebekah, the servant, and the ten camels traveled to Abraham and Isaac's home. *(Walk in place.)*

Isaac and Rebekah were married. They loved each other. *(Cross your hands over your heart.)*

Match the Twins

There are many different children pictured, but only two of the children are identical twins. Circle the identical twins.

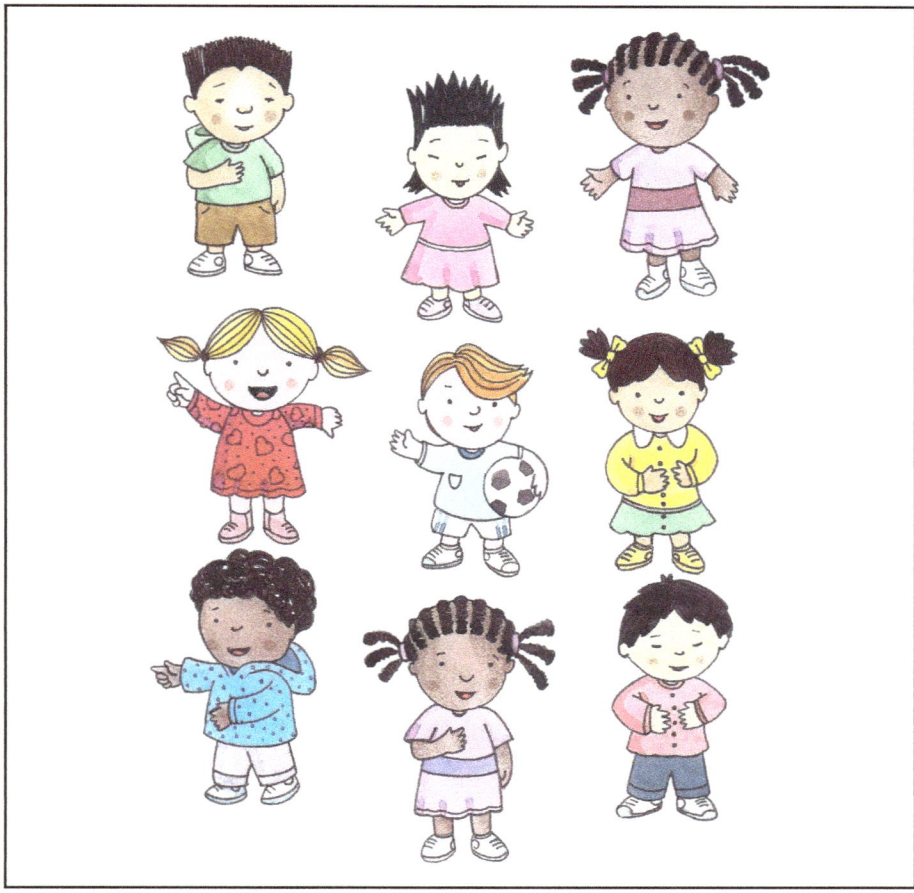

Talk About It

Use these questions to talk about today's Bible story with your child.

- How do you think Rebekah felt when she found out she was having twins?
- How are you different from other members of your family? How are you the same?

PRAY: Thank you, God, for blessing us. Amen.

Jacob and Esau

Genesis 25:19-28

Every family of earth will be blessed because of you and your descendants.
Genesis 28:14

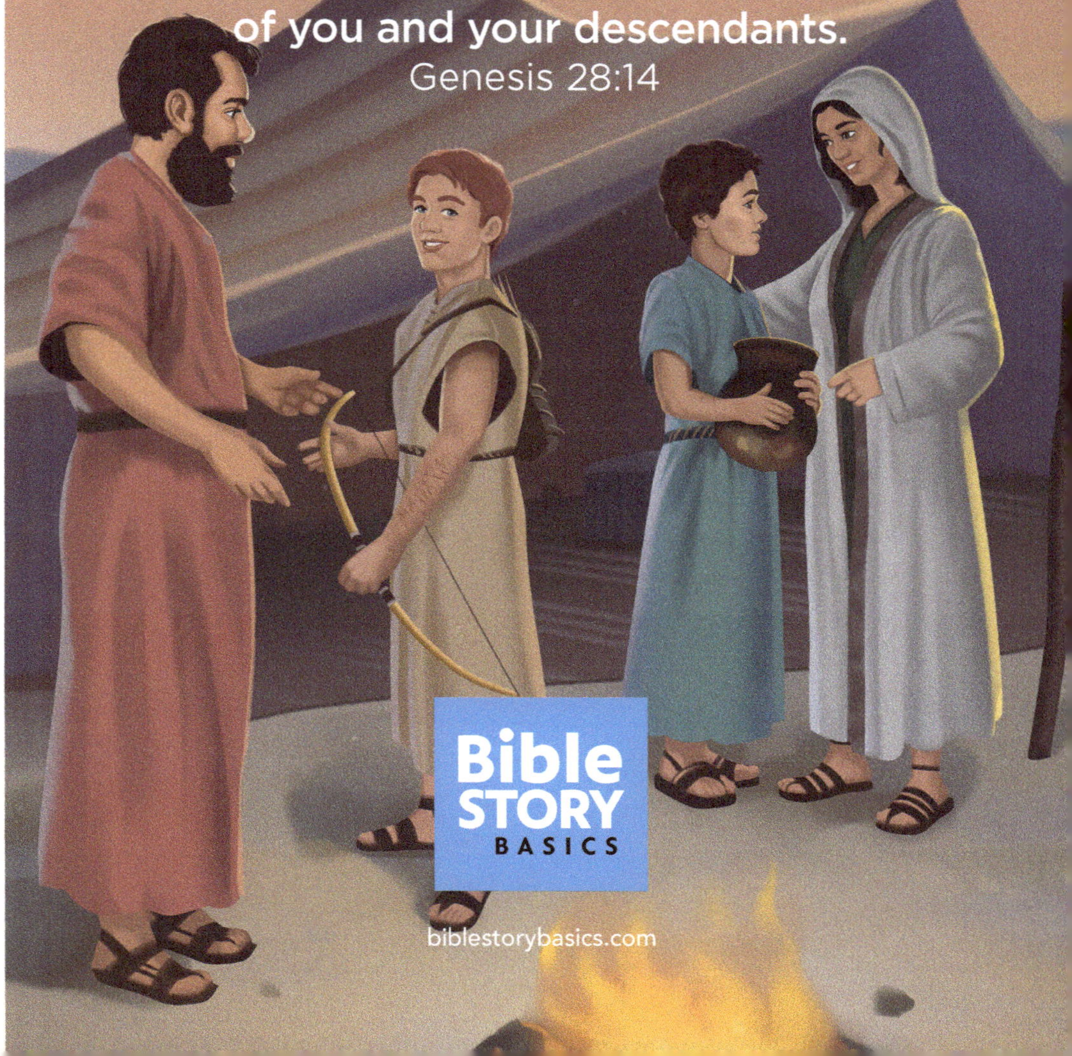

Bible STORY BASICS

biblestorybasics.com

Jacob and Esau

Isaac and Rebekah were married, but they did not have any children. After many, many years, Rebekah found out she was going to have TWO babies! Rebekah was going to have twins.

Two babies? Yes, that's right. *(Hold up two fingers; nod your head yes.)* **But they were as different as day and night.** *(Hold out one hand, then hold out the other hand.)*

The twins pushed and shoved at each other the whole time they were growing inside their mother.

Two babies? Yes, that's right. *(Hold up two fingers; nod your head yes.)* **But they were as different as day and night.** *(Hold out one hand, then hold out the other hand.)*

Finally, it was time for Rebekah's twins to be born. The first baby was a boy. Isaac and Rebekah named him Esau. His skin was red and hairy.

The second baby was also a boy. Isaac and Rebekah named him Jacob. His skin was very smooth.

Two babies? Yes, that's right. *(Hold up two fingers; nod your head yes.)* **But they were as different as day and night.** *(Hold out one hand, then hold out the other hand.)*

As the boys grew, Esau liked to be outdoors. He liked to hunt. Jacob liked to stay close to home. He liked to cook.

Two babies? Yes, that's right. *(Hold up two fingers; nod your head yes.)* **But they were as different as day and night.** *(Hold out one hand, then hold out the other hand.)*

The brothers were twins, but they were very different.

Two babies? Yes, that's right. *(Hold up two fingers; nod your head yes.)* **But they were as different as day and night.** *(Hold out one hand, then hold out the other hand.)*

What Belongs in Stew?

In our Bible story, Jacob made stew. Circle the things you think belong in stew. Cross out the things you think don't belong in stew.

Talk About It

Use these questions to talk about today's Bible story with your child.

- Do you think Esau made a good choice?
- How do you make good choices?

PRAY: Thank you, God, for blessing us. Amen.

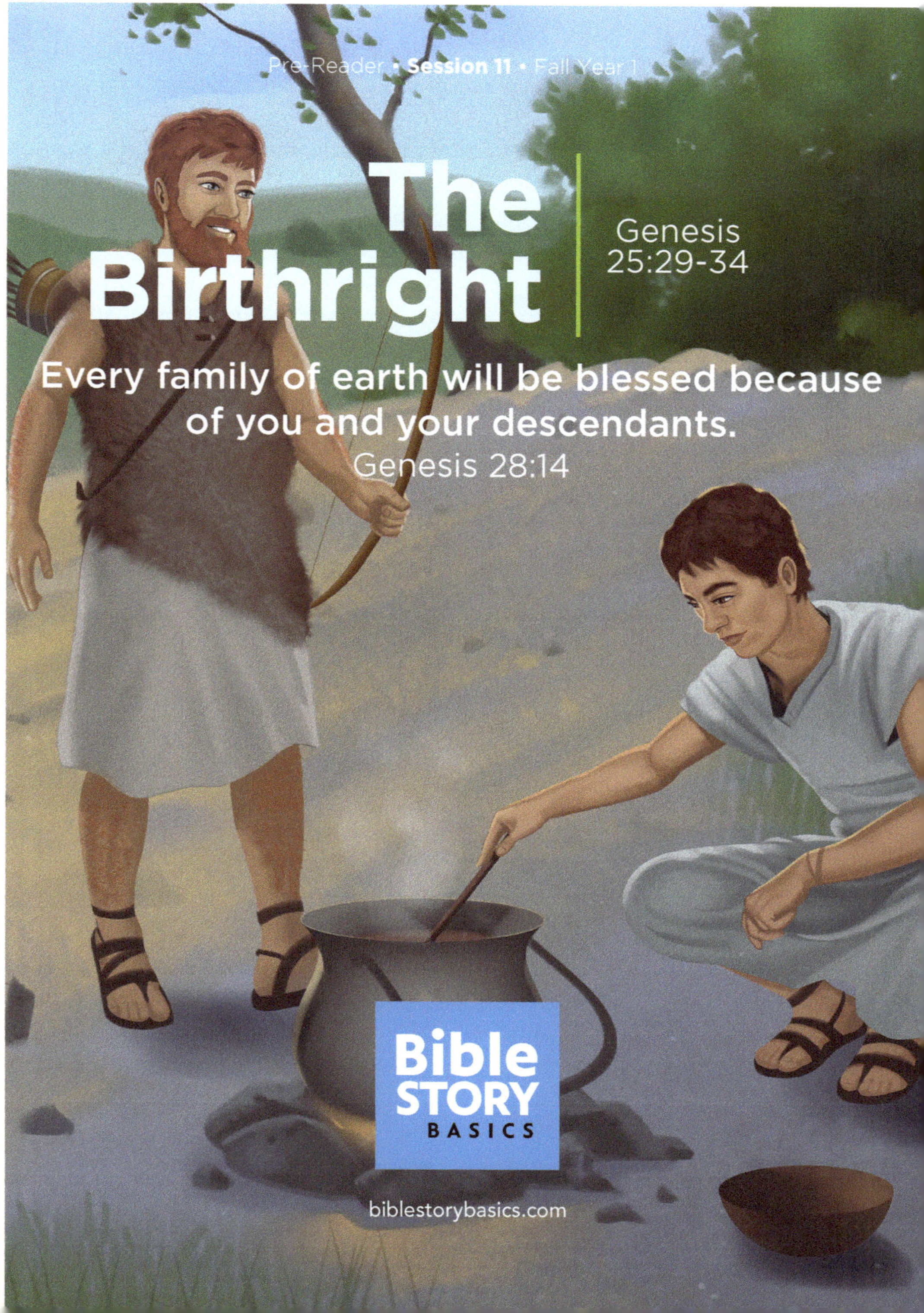

The Birthright

Genesis 25:29-34

Every family of earth will be blessed because of you and your descendants.
Genesis 28:14

BIBLE STORY BASICS

biblestorybasics.com

The Birthright

Isaac and Rebekah had twin baby boys. They named the boys **Esau** and **Jacob**.

Esau was born first, so he was the older son.

Jacob was born second, so he was the younger son.

Esau and **Jacob** grew, just like all babies grow. They kept growing until they were men. Even when they both became men, **Esau** was still the older son, and **Jacob** was still the younger son.

Because **Esau** was the older son, he was going to be the next leader of the family.

Esau also would get most of the family's tents, sheep, goats, camels, and money. This was called **Esau's** birthright.

Because **Jacob** was the younger son, he was not going to be the next leader of the family.

Jacob would get only a small number of the family's tents, sheep, goats, camels, and money.

But **Jacob** wanted to be the leader. He wanted the family's tents, sheep, goats, camels, and money. He wanted **Esau's** birthright.

One day, while **Esau** went hunting, **Jacob** stayed home and made stew. When **Esau** came back home, he saw **Jacob** making the stew. **Esau** was very hot, very tired, and very hungry.

"Give me some of that stew," **Esau** said to **Jacob**.

"I'll give you a bowl of stew," answered **Jacob**, "if you give me your birthright."

"What good is my birthright if I die from hunger?" asked **Esau**.

So, **Jacob** gave **Esau** a bowl of stew and some bread. **Esau** gave **Jacob** his birthright.

Now **Jacob** would be the leader of the family. **Jacob** would get most of the family's tents, sheep, goats, camels, and money.

Touch It

Jacob wore fur on his arms to trick Isaac. Circle the pictures of things that are furry.

Talk About It

Use these questions to talk about today's Bible story with your child.

- How do you think Jacob felt when his father gave him the blessing?
- How do you think Esau felt when he found out Jacob had tricked Isaac out of the blessing?

PRAY: Thank you, God, for blessing us. Amen.

Pre-Reader • **Session 12** • Fall Year 1

The Blessing
Genesis 27:1-46

Every family of earth will be blessed because of you and your descendants.
Genesis 28:14

Bible STORY BASICS

biblestorybasics.com

The Blessing

Isaac had grown very old and could no longer see very well. *(Point to your eyes.)*

He could tell which son was Esau and which son was Jacob only by touching their arms. Esau had hairy arms, and Jacob had smooth ones. *(Rub your arms.)*

One day, Isaac spoke to Esau. *(Cup hands around mouth.)*

"Esau," said Isaac, "you are my older son. It is time I give you my blessing so you can be the next leader of our family." *(Place your fingertips on your forehead.)*

Rebekah heard what Isaac said to Esau. She did not want Esau to be the next leader of the family. *(Shake your head no.)* Rebekah wanted Jacob to be the leader. *(Nod your head yes.)*

Rebekah came up with a plan to trick Isaac into giving Jacob the blessing. *(Place your fingertips on your forehead.)*

Rebekah cooked Isaac's favorite meal. *(Pretend to eat.)*

Next, Rebekah wrapped fur on Jacob's arms to make them hairy, like Esau's arms. *(Rub your arms.)*

Then Jacob gave the food to Isaac. *(Walk in place.)*

"Let me touch you," said Isaac. "Are you Esau or Jacob?" *(Rub your arms.)*

"I'm Esau," lied Jacob, as Isaac touched Jacob's fur-covered arms. *(Rub your arms.)*

So, Isaac gave Jacob the special blessing that made Jacob the leader of the family. *(Place your fingertips on your forehead.)*

Esau was really mad when he found out Isaac had given Jacob the special blessing meant for him. *(Stomp your feet.)*

Rebekah was afraid Esau would hurt Jacob, so she told Jacob to go away for a while. *(Point to the distance.)*

Jacob quickly left home so he would be safe. *(Walk in place.)*

Match the Angels

Jacob dreamed he saw angels walking up and down a staircase. Draw a line connecting each pair of matching angels.

Talk About It

Use these questions to talk about today's Bible story with your child.

- How do you think Jacob felt when he woke up from his dream?
- How does it make you feel to know God is always with you?

PRAY: Thank you, God, for blessing us. Amen.

Pre-Reader • **Session 13** • Fall Year 1

Jacob's Dream
Genesis 28:10-22

Every family of earth will be blessed because of you and your descendants.
Genesis 28:14

Bible STORY BASICS

biblestorybasics.com

Jacob's Dream

Esau was mad! *(Stomp your feet.)*

Jacob had tricked their father, Isaac, into giving Jacob the blessing meant for Esau. *(Place your fingertips on your forehead.)*

Now Jacob would be the leader of the family, not Esau. *(Shake your head no.)*

Their mother, Rebekah, was afraid Esau would hurt Jacob, so she told Jacob to go away for a while. *(Point to the distance.)*

Jacob quickly left home so he would be safe. *(Walk in place.)*

Jacob walked and walked. *(Walk in place.)*

Finally, the sun started going down. It was getting dark. *(Hold your hands in a circle over your head, then bring your arms down.)*

Jacob stopped. He was so tired that he lay down on the ground to sleep. He used a rock for his pillow. *(Press your hands together, and rest your cheek on your hands.)*

While Jacob was sleeping, he had a dream. In his dream, he saw a staircase going all the way to the sky. *(Reach up to the sky.)*

Angels walked up and down the stairs. *(Flap your arms like wings.)*

God spoke from the staircase. *(Cup your hands around your mouth.)*

"I'll give you and your family the land you are lying on," said God. "Every family on earth will be blessed because of you and your children. I promise that I will always be with you." *(Cross your hands over your heart.)*

Jacob woke up. *(Stretch your arms as if you are waking up.)*

"It is good to know that God is with me," said Jacob. *(Cross your hands over your heart.)*

Pray

Color the praying hands. Say a prayer of thanks to God for God's never-ending love.

Talk About It

Use these questions to talk about Thanksgiving with your child.

- What are three things you are thankful for?
- What is your favorite thing about Thanksgiving?

PRAY: Thank you, God, for all the wonderful things you have done for us. Amen.

Pre-Reader • **Thanksgiving Send-Home** • Fall Year 1

Happy Thanksgiving!

Thanksgiving is a great time to give thanks to God. The Psalms have many verses that help us say thank you to God. You can find the Book of Psalms in the middle of your Bible.

Give thanks to the Lord because he is good, because his faithful love lasts forever!
Psalm 107:1

Bible STORY BASICS

biblestorybasics.com

Thank God

Trace and color the hearts in the picture.

I will thank you, Lord, with all my heart;
I will talk about all your wonderful acts.
Psalm 9:1

With All Your Heart

Follow the path to the center of the heart.

I give thanks to you with all my heart, Lord.
Psalm 138:1

Hear Us As We Pray

Your children will sing this song each week before prayer time. Sing the song with your family before praying.

Lord, we call to you right now.
Hear us as we pray.

Folded hands and quiet hearts
Hear us as we pray.

Give us heroes' hearts.
Reveal your truth today.
Give us strength to do what's good.
Hear us as we pray.
Hear us as we pray.

Lord, we ask this in your name.
Hear us as we pray.

Boldly share, your truth proclaim.
Hear us as we pray.

Give us heroes' hearts
To live your truth each day.
Give us courage in our faith.
Hear us as we pray.
Hear us as we pray.

Lord, we call to you right now.
Hear us as we pray.

Guide our feet and light our way.
Hear us as we pray.

Give us heroes' hearts
In all we do and say.
Give us hope as we seek peace.
Hear us as we pray.
Hear us as we pray.

Hear us as we pray.

Words: Matt Huesmann
Music: Matt Huesmann

© 2017 Matt Huesmann Music. Used by permission. All rights reserved.

Pre-Reader • Songbook Take-Home • Fall Year 1

Bible Story Basics Songbook

Sing these songs with your children to help them remember the Bible stories.

biblestorybasics.com

Our God Made All the Earth Spin

Tune: "She'll Be Coming 'Round the Mountain"

Oh, our God made all the earth spin 'round the sun.
Oh, our God made all the earth spin 'round the sun.
Oh, our God made all the earth spin; oh, our God made all the earth spin;
Oh, our God made all the earth spin 'round the sun.

God Made

Tune: "Ring Around the Rosie"

So, God made the first man,
(Walk around the circle.)
The first man, the first man.
So, God made the first man,
And Adam was his name.
(All fall down.)

Then God made a garden,
(Walk around the circle.)
A garden, a garden.
Then God made a garden,
And Eden was its name.
(All fall down.)

Then God made a woman,
(Walk around the circle.)
A woman, a woman.
Then God made a woman,
And Eve was her name.
(All fall down.)

God Called Abraham

Tune: "Are You Sleeping?" ("Frère Jacques")

God called Abraham, God called Abraham.
"Go this way. Go this way.
"To a land I show you. To a land I show you.
"Go today. Go today."

Isaac and Rebekah Had Two Sons

Tune: "She'll Be Coming 'Round the Mountain"

Oh, Isaac and Rebekah had two sons.
Oh, Isaac and Rebekah had two sons.
Oh, the first son was named Esau, and the second was named Jacob.
Oh, Isaac and Rebekah had two sons.

Jacob Had a Dream

Tune: "The Farmer in the Dell"

Oh, Jacob had a dream.
(Press your hands together, and rest your cheek on your hands.)
Oh, Jacob had a dream.
As he slept upon the ground,
(Touch the ground.)
Oh, Jacob had a dream.
(Press your hands together, and rest your cheek on your hands.)

Oh, Jacob had a dream.
(Press your hands together, and rest your cheek on your hands.)
Oh, Jacob had a dream.
He saw a staircase to heaven.
(Stretch your arms up high over your head.)
Oh, Jacob had a dream.
(Press your hands together, and rest your cheek on your hands.)

Oh, Jacob had a dream.
(Press your hands together, and rest your cheek on your hands.)
Oh, Jacob had a dream.
There were angels on the staircase.
(Wave your arms like angel wings.)
Oh, Jacob had a dream.
(Press your hands together, and rest your cheek on your hands.)

Oh, Jacob had a dream.
(Press your hands together, and rest your cheek on your hands.)
Oh, Jacob had a dream.
God spoke to Jacob in the dream.
(Shake your index finger.)
Oh, Jacob had a dream.
(Press your hands together, and rest your cheek on your hands.)

Oh, Jacob had a dream.
(Press your hands together, and rest your cheek on your hands.)
Oh, Jacob had a dream.
God said, "I'll always be with you."
(Point to yourself.)
Oh, Jacob had a dream.
(Press your hands together, and rest your cheek on your hands.)

Vol. 1 • No. 1 • Fall Year 1

EDITORIAL / DESIGN TEAM

Daphna Flegal	Writer/Editor
Lucas Hilliard	Production Editor
Jim Carlton	Designer

ADMINISTRATIVE TEAM

Rev. Brian K. Milford	President and Publisher
Marjorie M. Pon	Associate Publisher and Editor of Church School Publications
Mary M. Mitchell	Design Manager
Brittany Sky	Senior Editor, Children's Resources

BIBLE STORY BASICS: PRE-READER, BIBLE STORY LEAFLETS: An official resource for The United Methodist Church approved by Discipleship Ministries and published quarterly by Abingdon Press, a division of The United Methodist Publishing House, 2222 Rosa L. Parks Blvd., Nashville, TN 37228-1306. Price: $8.99. Copyright © 2019 Abingdon Press. All rights reserved. Send address changes to BIBLE STORY BASICS: PRE-READER, BIBLE STORY LEAFLETS, Subscription Services, 2222 Rosa L. Parks Blvd., Nashville, TN 37228-1306 or call 800-672-1789. Printed in China.

To order copies of this publication, call toll free: **800-672-1789**. You may fax your order to 800-445-8189. Telecommunication Device for the Deaf/Telex Telephone: 800-227-4091. Or order online at *cokesbury.com*. Use your Cokesbury account, American Express, Visa, Discover, or Mastercard.

For information concerning permission to reproduce any material in this publication, write to Rights and Permissions, The United Methodist Publishing House, 2222 Rosa L. Parks Blvd., Nashville, TN 37228-1306. You may fax your request to 615-749-6128. Or email *permissions@umpublishing.org*.

Scripture quotations are taken from the Common English Bible, copyright 2011. Used by permission. All rights reserved.

Cover design by Ed Maksimowicz. Illustrations by Ralph Voltz.

Art: pp. 1, 2, & 3 of Sessions 1–13, Parent Take-Home, Songbook Take-Home, Thanksgiving Send-Home: Ralph Voltz; p. 4 of Sessions 1, 4, 5, 12, 13, Parent Take-Home, Thanksgiving Send-Home: Shutterstock®; p. 4 of Session 2: Patrick Girouard/Portfolio Solutions; p. 4 of Session 3: Susan Jaekel/Ann Remen-Willis Rep.; p. 4 of Sessions 6, 8–9: Farida Zaman/Storybook Arts, Inc.; p. 4 of Session 7: Mary France/Gwen Walters Artist Rep.; p. 4 of Sessions 10–11: Alberto Lunghini/WendyLynn & Co.